PERSONAL EVANGELISM

How to lead people to Christ
Helping people follow Christ

BIBLE
MODULAR
SERIES

BJU PRESS
Greenville, South Carolina

This textbook was written by members of the faculty and staff of Bob Jones University. Standing for the "old-time religion" and the absolute authority of the Bible since 1927, Bob Jones University is the world's leading fundamental Christian university. The staff of the University is devoted to educating Christian men and women to be servants of Jesus Christ in all walks of life.

Providing unparalleled academic excellence, Bob Jones University prepares its students through its offering of over 120 majors, while its fervent spiritual emphasis prepares their minds and hearts for service and devotion to the Lord Jesus Christ.

If you would like more information about the spiritual and academic opportunities available at Bob Jones University, please call **1-800-BJ-AND-ME (1-800-252-6363)**. *www.bju.edu*

NOTE:
The fact that materials produced by other publishers may be referred to in this volume does not constitute an endorsement of the content or theological position of materials produced by such publishers. Any references and ancillary materials are listed as an aid to the student or the teacher and in an attempt to maintain the accepted academic standards of the publishing industry.

Personal Evangelism and Discipleship

Coart Ramey, M.A.; James A. Berg, M.A.; Stephen Hankins, Ph.D.
©1999 BJU Press
Greenville, South Carolina 29614

Printed in the United States of America
All rights reserved

ISBN 978-1-57924-304-3

15   14   13   12   11   10   9   8   7   6   5   4

CONTENTS

Introduction

The small group of plainly dressed men watched politely as one of their number stepped behind the rough wooden pulpit. He announced the topic of his sermon in that simple, calm manner he always used when preaching. The title, "An Inquiry into the Obligation of Christians to Use Means for the Conversion of the Heathen," piqued the audience's interest. It implied that William thought Christian people should be taking it upon themselves to teach the heathen about God!

That truly was a surprising message from a preacher in William's day. Good Christian people of that period believed that God would convert the "heathen" whenever He pleased. Did the Bible not teach as much? While pouring much time and thought into studying his Bible, William had realized that God says *Christians* are to tell unsaved people about Christ without waiting for a special sign or event. God has issued standing orders to all His people to tell the heathen about Jesus Christ.

William, whose last name was Carey, became the first figure in a tide of British missionaries that spread around the world during the next 150 years. Why was telling unsaved people about Christ such a novel thought until William's sermon? People in earlier centuries had shared the gospel freely. The problem in William Carey's eighteenth-century England was that virtually everyone called himself a Christian. Everyone knew what a Christian was. If you would have asked a woman on the street if she were trusting Jesus Christ for salvation, she would have certainly replied "yes," and probably been irritated that you even asked.

It is not that the British were all truly saved the Bible way; on the contrary, many did not really understand the gospel. They called themselves Christian whether or not they were genuinely saved.

In a society of nominal Christians, the true Christians find it difficult to keep telling others about Christ. The gospel seems like old news. It is much easier to carry on the routine Christian life without deliberately evangelizing unsaved people.

But no one even claimed to be a Christian in India, the place where Carey wanted to evangelize the lost. By studying his Bible,

William Carey realized God wants His people to take the gospel to the heathen—people who have never heard it. God's will for English Christians had been the same in the years before Carey lived, but few had understood and obeyed it as Carey did.

Are the people in your area Christians, nominal Christians, or heathens? True Christians are rarely a majority. What percentage of teenagers and adults go to a church, any church, on Sunday mornings? How many of those churches teach the gospel as the Bible teaches it? Most of the people in your neighborhood and town are probably a mixture of nominal Christians and heathens who would not even claim Christianity.

So why bother being a Christian? After all, if it is not popular to be a *real* Christian, why even go to the trouble? Real Christians obey the Bible, and the Bible says Christians are supposed to tell other people how to become Christians. All those people in your town are happy remaining as they are. They do not need you to tell them how to be happy or go to heaven. You will do them more good by just showing what a good person you are and by having a positive influence on society.

Right?

If no one has ever said those words to you, just wait; someone will. Most nominal Christians believe those ideas are true. naturally, nominal Christians call themselves real Christians. They think reasoning and common sense show that Christians have no business trying to evangelize those who do not want to be evangelized. Consequently, they slide unknowingly toward the kind of culture in which William Carey lived in England, a culture in which everyone assumes everyone else either is a Christian or would become one if he cared to.

What are your own feelings about sharing the gospel of Jesus Christ with others? If you honestly have no desire to tell others what Christ has done to save them, please carefully consider your own relationship with Him. When you recognize the plain facts of what the Lord Jesus did for you to save you from your sin, you ought to at least acknowledge your debt to Him. What is more, if you have trusted the Lord to save you, you and He are now friends. As His friend, you should be steadily learning more about Him and how you can please Him.

So how does pleasing Christ relate to telling other people about Him? You say, "Because Christ is pleased when I tell people about Him. Sure, sure. I've heard that one plenty of times." But why is He so pleased when you share the gospel? God is pleased because he sees it as a sacrifice from a loving heart. If you love the Lord, it is only natural to want to tell other people about Him. The problem is that witnessing is *hard!*

William Carey pioneered the Baptist Missionary Society in 1792.

William Carey had no idea what difficulties would confront him. He knew what was right, and he knew what God specifically wanted him to do. But the price he eventually paid to be a missionary to India was higher than he could have guessed—the work was very slow, he was often sick, and his wife became mentally ill. The small group of pastors that had gathered to listen to his sermon were the first ones to give money to support Carey's endeavor. They were very poor men. It took great sacrifice for them to send one family around the world. In India, the gospel was not a welcome message. Carey endured many hardships during his years there. Many of the Indians for whom he had given up so much to help wanted nothing to do with Jesus Christ.

Was William Carey right? Why is it necessary to put forth so much time and effort to evangelize the lost? If it were *easy,* you would happily choose to evangelize whenever the opportunity arose. But since it is contrary to your own sinful nature and offensive to every human's inherent sin and pride, evangelizing is (and always will be) *difficult.* Going to the trouble and expense to do what is difficult shows our love for Christ much more than doing an easy task.

The question we have to answer is, "Why is it difficult to turn lost people to Christ?" In answering this question, we will learn why so many people who say they are Christians are not, why evangelism costs so much time and money, and why you find it so much easier not to tell others about Christ.

William Carey became a great missionary, one who left his home country to spread the gospel in another country. This is not a book about missionaries, but it is about the work they and all Christians must do to make other people good disciples of the Lord Jesus Christ.

A *disciple* is a follower, a student who becomes like his master. As a Christian, you are Christ's disciple, and your lifetime task is to make more disciples for Him. Making disciples is the best way to show Him your gratitude—and it is the greatest service you can render another human being!

CHAPTER ONE

Turning a Rebel into a Disciple

①

Memory Verses: Matthew 28:18-20

Introduction

This course is about the part you play as a Christian in turning a sinner into a faithful child of God. The Lord is working actively throughout the world, drawing people to trust Christ and then grow as Christians. He has you act as His messenger. The message He sends through you is the entire Bible—telling people both how to be saved (the gospel) and what to do after being saved.

Thus there are two halves to your part in turning sinners into disciples:

- telling them how to be saved

- teaching them what God expects of a saved person

Consequently, there are two errors to avoid:

- considering your responsibility completed after leading someone to the Lord

- waiting passively for people to get saved on their own and then come to you to learn about the Bible

Instead, we must envision bringing unsaved people all the way from being rebels against God to being fruitful, joyful children of God. In this first chapter, we want to learn why sin makes discipleship difficult, how Christ wants us to make sinners into disciples, and what will happen to them if we do not.

What Sin Really Is

Let's look at the first chapter of Ezekiel. When you approach someone to tell him about Christ, you will be doing what God's children have done plenty of times before. Ezekiel lived in a time in which many people claimed to serve God but did not obey His Word.

Ezekiel was a Jew, one of God's chosen race. God gave the Jews a country of their own. Through repeated rebellion against God's law and rejection of His prophets, the Jews brought punishment on themselves and lost their country. God allowed another very evil nation, Babylon, to conquer and rule over the Jews.

Mesopotamia

Though in exile from the land God gave them, the Jews still would not repent of their sin but continued in rebellion against the Lord. God called Ezekiel to be yet another prophet proclaiming His warning to the people.

Read the first four verses of Ezekiel. Chapter 1 contains Ezekiel's description of his vision of the throne of God in heaven. He saw things that sound strange to us: multifaced, winged creatures; colossal chariot wheels; and the figure of God on His throne. Ezekiel was struggling to put heavenly things into earthly words. God let him see for a few moments heavenly realities. The wheels and living creatures are God's angelic servants; their shapes and forms help display that God's presence and power are spread across the whole earth. The vision was not for Ezekiel's entertainment; it was the basis for what God was about to tell Ezekiel to do.

Put yourself in Ezekiel's sandals as he hears the Lord's command. You told the Lord years ago you would do whatever He wanted, but now that His order has come, you wonder what you've gotten yourself into. Not that you really had a choice; as He is about to demonstrate, God rules all men whether they willingly submit to Him or not!

Read chapter 2:3-5. Notice that there is one phrase to describe Israel and two verbs to define the nation's actions. The phrase is *a rebellious nation*. One verb is *hath rebelled* and the other is *have transgressed*. Was the problem that the people did not know God? The problem was not ignorance but rebellion. **Rebellion** is a willful refusal to obey authority. The Israelites had received more knowledge about God than any other people in history, but despite all they knew about God, they refused to believe it and act on it. Like the nominal Christians in William Carey's England, all of them claimed to follow the true God, but few cared what His Word really said.

The people of Israel not only refused to obey God but were actively disobeying Him. It is not possible to be neutral. Either we do what God commands, or we do what He forbids. The people of Israel "have transgressed," says the Lord in verse 3. **Transgression** is going out of set bounds; it is moving into an off-limits area. Its most basic meaning is leaving a road to wander off into a field. Crossing out of bounds when dribbling a basketball is the same idea. When God uses the word in a moral context, as in Ezekiel 2, the real meaning of sin shows itself. *Sin is rebellion and transgression*. A sinner refuses to do what God says (rebellion) and au-

tomatically does what God forbids (transgression).

What is the attitude of people you know who say they are Christians but act like unsaved people? How do they react when you show them that genuine Christians have lives changed by the truth? They probably act as the Jews did. Look at the two descriptions of them in verse 4: *impudent children* and *stiffhearted*. *Impudence* is an offensive boldness, like a child who stares you in the eye and dares you to spank him.

Stiff here is from a word that means strong or hard, able to resist and defeat opposition, like the strength of a wrestler or the strength of an army. The *heart* is what we often call the mind, the inner person encompassing our thinking, feeling, and decision making. A person with a stiff heart, then, *refuses to agree that he is wrong, refuses to feel any remorse or guilt, and refuses to change his actions.*

Did God assure Ezekiel of results? Verse 5 contains the conditional phrase "Whether . . . or . . ."; God does not promise the preacher that people will believe what he says. He says only that they will eventually know that they have heard the truth! Although the Lord knows in advance how people will respond to His message, He does not tell His messengers what the response will be. When you say to someone, "God is real and living, and He wants you to stop sinning and personally trust Him for your salvation," do you expect that person to instantly drop to his knees in sorrowful repentance?

Read verses 6 and 7 to see what Ezekiel could expect. Does it sound like a fun life? Notice especially the two things Ezekiel was not to fear. When you present the truth to people who are content in their sin, you are guaranteed to get two things: *tough looks* and *sharp words*. Imagine the look that says, "When you grow up, you'll realize life isn't so simple." Or imagine a teen who looks at you as if you were a Martian. Like it or not, looks from others do have a powerful effect on us. It takes real courage to tell a man the truth when the truth hurts.

Worse than tough looks are sharp words. The cliché about sticks and stones breaking what words cannot is deceptive. At your age, you know full well that words strike home in a way punches never do. People may mock you, belittle you, or humiliate you when you try to do them the biggest favor of their lives. God Almighty told Ezekiel to get ready for it.

Read the command in verse 8. Ezekiel still had a free will to disobey the Lord. The temptation to abandon God's work is strong and persistent. Ezekiel would have needed to make a habit of overcoming that temptation, for he was being called to a life's work—not a temporary thrill. He spent more than twenty years preaching to Israel.

Contrast William Carey with Ezekiel as you read verses 4 through 6. Have you ever thought of foreign missions as an easier task than ministering to the people around you? It is possible for a people who have heard the truth over and over to become so hardened that they are more difficult to reach than pagans!

Ezekiel 3:7 answers the question "Why do people not listen to a preacher of God's Word?" Divide the verse into three parts according to its punctuation. The word *for* in this verse means "because." Therefore, the first sentence makes a statement, the second sentence gives a reason for the first statement, and the third sentence gives a reason for the second statement. We can reverse the order of the sentences and write *therefore* between each pair to clarify this verse: "All the house of Israel are impudent and hardhearted; *therefore* they will not hearken unto me; *therefore* they will not hearken unto you." People do not listen to God because they willfully rebel against Him; they *will not* obey. People do not listen to God's messengers because they will not listen to God.

Strong in the next verse is the same word as *stiff* in 2:4. God promises to give the prophet power to be as firm as the people are rebellious, as hardheaded as they are stubborn. An adamant is a

---

Cookbook

From 2:9 to 3:3 Ezekiel writes that God actually had him eat a scroll. This was a symbolic act signifying that God put His own words in Ezekiel's mouth. God's message was full of sorrow (verse 10), but it tasted sweet to the prophet. That shows that it was not a literal book, because books do not taste good. (You are invited to eat part of this page if you doubt it.) You do not have to eat a spiritual book; Ezekiel did that for you and wrote it all down. His reward was becoming a Bible hero, but you get the privilege of learning God's words the easy way.

very hard substance. Imagine the look you would get from a police officer who had seen you obviously breaking a traffic regulation. Be stubborn and argue all you want; his face will be set in stone.

In verses 10 to 17 of chapter three, the Lord commands Ezekiel to go speak to the people. Ezekiel hears the noise of the living creatures and the big wheels and then finds himself filled with righteous anger and transported to the place where many Israelites are living.

Read Ezekiel 3:17-21 before continuing. The chart below summarizes the passage.

This admonition clearly implies some responsibility on the messenger's part; that is, a wicked man might have turned from sin had he been warned, and a righteous man might have avoided sin if he had been warned. We know that God chooses sinners to salvation, but this passage teaches unambiguously the parallel truth that *humans are responsible for their own obedience.*

What We Do About It: The Great Commission

We have seen that the great obstacle to evangelism and discipleship is human sin. People do not trust Christ because they do not want to; they like being sinners. So what do we do about it? The Lord Jesus outlined our task and the proper method for accomplishing it in the Great Commission.

After the Lord Jesus Christ completed His ministry on earth, He led His disciples to the top of a mountain and gave them the charge we call the Great Commission (Matt. 28:18-20). What had just happened? Only days earlier, Christ had risen alive from the dead. He who was by outward appearance a normal man had been executed as a criminal. Now He was alive again. No miracle could match that, especially when we consider that His death was not the death of an ordinary man, but that He died under the weight of God's wrath upon all human sin, suffering in an instant the justice that would have taken all mankind all of eternity to satisfy.

The risen Lord's first sentence in this passage to His disciples is "All power is given unto me in heaven and in earth." This is an incredible assertion for anyone. *Power* is properly the word *authority*, the power to rule by right. For example, the president of the United States may not be any larger or stronger than another American, but his authority is greater than any other by right of his office, giving him great "power."

Jesus had authority to give a command to the whole world. What He had commanded, was then commanding, and eventually commanded His disciples are equally His commands to us. By saying "in heaven," He shows that He is much more than an earthly king; His authority is imparted by God, from the Creator's absolute authority to do as He pleases. "On earth" shows that he is all an earthly king is but is unlimited by distance or location. He supersedes human rulers by right.

The Ascension by Benjamin West P.R.A.

What is the primary command in the Great Commission? Is it "Go"? "Go" is really a participle, that sets the stage for the rest of the sentence. In the verse the participle could be translated "having gone." The words *baptizing* and *teaching* are also participles. The only imperative verb is *teach*, and it is a different word than the participle *teaching* in verse 20. Its root word is the same as *disciple*, as in one of the eleven disciples standing there to hear this Great Commission (v. 16). As a verb, it means "to make someone into a disciple." The object of this verb "make disciples," is "all nations." The Lord says to make disciples of all nations. Does the English word *of* mean to make all nations into disciples? No, it means to make disciples out of all the nations. That is, some people out of every nation on earth were to be made into disciples of Christ *by* His other disciples.

Acts 8:2-4 shows that the early Christians discipled. *Make disciples* means "to bring into a master-follower relationship." We make people Christ's disciples, not our own disciples. We cause them to learn from and imitate Christ Jesus.

In apostolic days, it was truly incredible to say that one religion was meant for the whole world! Religion was very much a racial or regional characteristic. Each country had its own religion with its own gods. There was little thought of proselytizing; the Romans simply swept any new god they heard of into their pantheon (meaning "many gods") and considered him one of the divine family. The Romans did not consider any one god absolutely superior. Much less did they imagine there could be *only* one God who had all power and authority and who deserved everyone's worship. Even the Jews, who should have known better, had become racially and religiously bigoted, thinking that they pleased God just by being Jews and that no one born to a different nation could ever please God as they could.

Information Service, Rome

The entrance to the Roman Pantheon, a temple dedicated to the worship of many gods

Two participles described the actions that had to accompany making disciples. Christ's disciples had to do these two things to make others into disciples. The first was *baptizing. Baptism is the one-time sign of commitment, transformation, change of direction, and new life.* It is a Christian's way of telling the world that Christ has saved him. Baptism is one commandment of Christ that every disciple must obey. This does not mean a person's salvation is dependent on baptism, for baptism is an outward sign of a spiritual reality. It is no more necessary to salvation than teaching is necessary to salvation; you do not have to learn all there is to know before you can be saved. But a true disciple will want to be baptized. He must be baptized to obey Christ perfectly.

What does baptism "in the name of" mean? The name of someone is simply a representation of that person. It is a more formal way of stating something about a person. God refers to His name as representing Himself many times in Scripture. When an ambassador acts in the name of the United States, he means he is the representative of the United States; he is acting on the country's behalf and with its authority.

Baptism is a picture, a symbol of at least two spiritual realities:

1. Purification, or cleansing from sin (Acts 22:16, I Pet. 3:21). Throughout the Old and the New Testaments, washing with water represents cleansing from sin's defilement.

2. Union with Christ in His burial and resurrection (Rom. 6:3ff., Gal. 3:27).

Baptism is also an oath of loyalty to God. By being baptized in His name, we show our pledge to forever follow Him and do as He commands. Baptism has long been the best-known public symbol of a person's commitment to Christ.

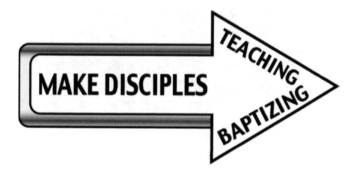

Teaching is the continual function of a disciple maker. Making another person like Christ requires *deliberate, systematic instruction in everything Christ taught.* Not only the Gospels but all the Bible is the teaching of Christ. Furthermore, we do not teach people just what the commandments are; we teach them to "observe" all those commandments. The word *observe* does not mean merely to look at, the way we use it today. It means to do a repeated action that was commanded. For example, "observing" the Sabbath means to do what God said to do on the Sabbath for every Sabbath.

Teaching people to observe Christ's commandments means that we teach them HOW to obey all those commandments and that they must obey them continually. Christ's commands are just that—commands. They are not optional for anyone. To make a man into a disciple is to teach him what he must do in his own life to obey all the commands Christ gives.

Finally, the Lord calls attention (*Lo!* means "Hey!" or "Listen!") to His last promise, the pledge to accompany His disciples to the end of the age. His "I" is emphatic, so there is no question He is saying that He personally will accompany them as they go into all nations of the world. He does not mean the Holy Spirit, though the Spirit certainly does go with us; rather, He promises to be with us Himself.

Alway is literally "all the days," or a promise that Christ is accompanying each of His disciples through every particular day. That stretch of days goes unto the end of *the age*, the age in which the church on earth is obeying His command to make disciples of all nations. Wherever any believer goes on any day of the entire Church Age, Christ assures that He personally is with that believer. Just as the Lord's universal absolute authority is the basis on which He gives such a command, so the promise of His perpetual presence is the assurance He will accomplish through our obedience what He intends.

What If We Don't?: Eternal Punishment

Will God really punish people who refuse to believe the gospel? Sin, at its root, is rebellion against the Lord, a willful rejection of His way. What becomes of those who will not turn from their own way, the wicked way? Is there another chance given to them in the next life? What about pagans dying in foreign lands who never heard a missionary? Did they get a different kind of chance to believe while they were on earth, or do they get a chance to believe right after death?

Does God eventually save everyone? Does the Bible exclude the possibility that God will save everyone eventually? Or does God destroy wicked people entirely, so there really is no "eternal suffering"?

What is hell like? Is it a place of oblivion, a place of regret and tortured conscience, or a physical place? Are there different levels of punishment for different people? Can you reduce your time in hell? Is hell ruled by the Devil and his demons? These are all good questions with which people have struggled for centuries. We dare not base our answers to them merely on what we think or "feel" is true; as with all other issues of eternal consequence, we must go to God's Word to learn the truth.

The Old Testament says a lot about God's wrath. We see a few references to the fact that punishment for rebelling against God is eternal, but mostly God pictures His wrath in the way He destroys His enemies on earth. For example, the way He judged Sodom and Gomorrah establishes His most prominent tool of judgment—fire (Gen. 19:24). Brimstone is sulfur, an element that burns at a lower temperature than most metals. God probably used sulfur because it is a common, cheap substance that most everyone in the ancient world was familiar with. It is not that the sulfur is not real; we have every reason to take this as literal burning sulfur falling onto the cities. It would probably have produced an effect like a huge bomb striking and destroying both cities in a massive, white-hot blast.

The Old Testament does indicate that the penalty for being God's enemy is eternal punishment. The prophet Isaiah warned people of God's terrible wrath in chapter 33, verse 14, when he said, "The sinners in Zion [Jerusalem] are afraid; fearfulness hath surprised the hypocrites. Who among us shall dwell with the devouring fire? who among us shall dwell with everlasting burnings?"

Isaiah's strongest passage on eternal punishment is located at the very end of his sixty-six-chapter book. Read Isaiah 66:15-24. This passage is set in the future, when the Lord will rule the new heaven and new earth directly. Verse 17 describes sins related to idolatry, while verse 19 shows that the whole world will acknowledge the Lord as God.

Halfway Hells

The Roman Catholic Church teaches that most people who were baptized go to purgatory after death. Purgatory is a place of limited suffering; a soul stays there until it is purged of all the sin the person committed but did not experience forgiveness for while he was alive. Buddhism teaches there are fourteen different hells, seven hot and seven cold, through which a person may move if he is too bad during his earthly incarnations. Neither of these views is supported by Scripture.

The final verse grips us by claiming that those who worship God forever will be able to see the bodies of people who never repented of sin. The description of unquenchable fire and an undying worm very likely was an allusion to the massive garbage disposal area in the valley of Ben-Hinnom, where Israelites burned their garbage with a continuous fire. The steady supply of garbage kept the fires from ever completely dying out. What the fire did not destroy, worms ate. Imagine how much the worms would have to eat in a place where flowed an endless stream of rotten food, the carcasses of dead animals, and other assorted wastes! Thus, the valley of Ben-Hinnom was a very visible picture of the eternal destiny of people who died in rebellion against God.

Photo by Bryan Smith

The Valley of Ben-Hinnom (Gehenna)

Some people find a measure of comfort about the afterlife by believing that sinners sent to hell are destroyed there. Yes, they say, hell may be a horrible place, but souls sent there will eventually cease to exist; their suffering will come to an end. But the New Testament makes it undeniable that hell is a place of endless suffering. The Lord Jesus Himself, who said so much about the love and mercy of God, who died in the place of sinners and rose again so that they might avoid hell and live forever with God, preached on the horrors of hell many times. In Mark 9:47-48 the Lord quoted Isaiah 66:24. Christ taught in Matthew 18:8 and 25:41-46 that hell lasts forever. He says in Matthew 13:42 that people in hell suffer consciously.

Luke 16 contains the Lord's most vivid warning of hell. In the story of the rich man and Lazarus, the rich man, in hell, asks that Lazarus, in heaven, might wet his finger and touch the rich man's tongue, for, he says, "I am tormented in this flame." That tiny bit of relief is all the former master of much asks. He is awake, alert to suffering, and has his memory intact.

The Book of Revelation gives us a preview of what will happen at the end of the Church Age. First, chapter 20 describes the binding of Satan during a one-thousand-year period and the first resurrection. Read verses 2 through 6 of Revelation 20.

Verse 7 starts the description of the last phase in the long rebellion against God. Satan is released for his "little season" (v. 3) to deceive the nations of the world one more time and lead them to besiege Jerusalem, the city that has been the Lord's earthly headquarters during that thousand-year period. Although the account may make us expect a dramatic final battle, Scripture dispenses with this last, largest uprising in a single sentence at the end of verse 9. This verse gives the final picture of God's wrath. It is consistent with the other judgments by fire. Now there remains the grim reality pictured in all preceding judgments.

First, the Devil is thrown into the lake that burns with fire and brimstone. The Beast and the False Prophet, two human beings who have given themselves entirely to Satan's service, are already in the lake of fire, having been thrown there at the beginning of the thousand years (see Rev. 19:20, which says plainly they were thrown in alive). The two chief rebels have not been annihilated by the lake; they are still in it when Satan joins them. The final phrase in 20:10 cannot be more clear that suffering in the lake is unending and eternal.

Verses 11 to 15 then record the last judgment, the second resurrection. This includes all people who ever lived who were not saved by faith in Jesus Christ. With heaven and earth gone, there is nothing in the universe on which to focus attention except the great white throne on which the Judge sits. We know from John 5:21-23 and II Timothy 4:1 that He is the Lord Jesus Christ. He who died to save all men has the right and authority to condemn forever those who rebelled against Him and rejected His offer of salvation.

The Book of Life is opened. A book of life was a birth registry recording the names of all babies born in a city. This is God's Book of Life recording the name of every person born into His family. Other books, containing records of every person's life, are opened. People who do not accept the salvation Christ provides must be judged by their works, and these books tell of the evil they have done.

Have you ever met someone who considered himself good enough to get into heaven? Do you know people who imagine all their pluses and minuses weighed in a giant scale to see if their pluses will tip the balance and get them into heaven? These people will receive exactly the kind of evaluation they expect. However, they must measure up to God's standard of righteousness to merit heaven. This passage and many others show that no human being who has ever lived is good enough to earn God's favor and merit life in heaven. People who stand before God with only their own works will all see their minuses heavily outweigh their pluses, for they will learn that Isaiah 64:6 is true in saying that "all our righteousnesses are as filthy rags" to our holy God.

Review Questions

_____1. In Ezekiel 2, the word *stiff* carries the idea of physical strength.

_____2. No one is ever judged according to his works.

3. Why did God have Ezekiel eat a scroll?

4. What is the primary command in the Great Commission?

5. What verse discussed in the text makes it clearest that those thrown into the lake of fire suffer consciously forever?

_____6. What is the greatest reason that evangelism is difficult?
   A. It costs too much.
   B. It is not natural.
   C. Sinners cannot understand the gospel.
   D. Sinners do not think that they are sinners.

_____7. What is sin?

    A. A willful refusal to obey God's authority
    B. Going out of bounds and doing what God forbids
    C. Lots of repeated mistakes
    D. A and B

_____8. Which of these best explains Jesus' authority in Matthew 28:18?

    A. His right to tell everyone what to do
    B. His ability to do whatever He wants
    C. His position as the greatest earthly king
    D. None of these

_____9. Which of the following is clearly true of someone who claims to believe in Christ but refuses water baptism?

    A. He has not believed in the name of Christ.
    B. He is not fully obedient to Scripture.
    C. He is not really saved.
    D. He draws attention to the spiritual reality of baptism.

_____10. Which of the following is a true statement about water baptism?

    A. Water baptism is a Christian's public declaration that he belongs to God.
    B. Water baptism unites a believer to Christ.
    C. Water baptism removes sin.
    D. All of the above

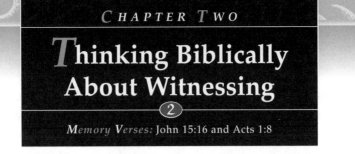

In this chapter and the next, we begin to study the first part of disciple making, personal evangelism. In Chapter 1 we laid the scriptural foundation for disciple making by examining what sin is like, what Christ said we should do for sinners, and what happens to sinners who never repent. With the biblical reasons for making disciples in mind, we want to discuss the skills and practical methods useful to that end.

Romans 10:13-14 teaches clearly that someone must hear the gospel in order to be saved. Though God saves people, He sends other people to *evangelize* them. To evangelize means "to proclaim the good message." God chooses to use imperfect men to proclaim the gospel because this method gives Him the opportunity to show His power in the midst of human weakness. Personal evangelism is telling someone that Christ died for his sins and wants him to repent of sin and be saved. Christians must tell others about Jesus Christ.

Part of this course requires you to practice personal evangelism. The particulars of personal evangelism change with circumstances. Witnessing to others about Christ is basically simple, but it is still a skill that improves with practice. You have to follow the scriptural principles in whatever way is most appropriate to your situation.

Chapters 2 and 3 are adapted from *Witnessing for Christ* by Stephen Hankins. Chapter 2 provides the proper scriptural mindset for personal evangelism and Chapter 3 outlines an excellent model to follow in an average witnessing encounter. As you read, imagine how the principles described will translate into real life as you go out to witness for Christ.

Introduction

Paul says, "For the preaching of the cross is to them that perish foolishness; but unto us which are saved it is the power of God" (I Cor. 1:18). There are two basic responses to the gospel of Christ. Some reject it because they view it as nonsense, and others accept it as the power of God to transform their lives. Christians, those who have been changed by the message of the cross, are obligated to present that message to others; they are representatives of Christ to a hostile world. Paul writes, "Now then we are ambassadors for Christ, as though God did beseech you by us: we pray you in Christ's stead, be ye reconciled to God" (II Cor. 5:20). Witnessing for Christ is not the responsibility of pastors and evangelists alone. Every believer is responsible to proclaim the good news of Christ. Note that in II Corinthians Paul addresses all Christians, not simply preachers.

The believer may be tempted to shun his responsibility to witness because of a fear of speaking or a fear of being rejected by others. But the believer must always remember that "God hath not given us the spirit of fear; but of power, and of love, and of a sound mind" (II Tim. 1:7). The believer must rest in the assurance of Acts 1:8, which states, "But ye shall receive power, after that the Holy Ghost is come upon you: and ye shall be witnesses unto me both in Jerusalem, and in all Judea, and in Samaria, and unto the uttermost part of the earth." The Lord will empower the believer to overcome the fear of speaking to others about Christ.

Accepting the reproach of the gospel is an essential part of being a faithful believer. Jesus says, "For whoever shall be ashamed of me and of my words, of him shall the Son of man be ashamed, when he shall come in his own glory, and in his Father's, and of the holy angels" (Luke 9:26). Believers cannot and should not try to avoid the reproach of Christ. Peter reminds us, "If ye be reproached for the name of Christ, happy are ye; for the spirit of glory and of God resteth upon you: on their part he is evil spoken of, but on your part he is glorified" (I Pet. 4:14).

I. The Importance of Witnessing

When something valuable is lost, men go to great lengths to find it. Mel Fisher, one of the greatest treasure hunters of the twentieth century, illustrates this truth. In 1969 Fisher formed Treasure Salvors, Inc., with family members, hired divers, and other assistants. They then began to search for the *Nuestra Señora de Atocha,* a Spanish galleon which sank near Key West during a hurricane in 1622. Reportedly, the galleon was carrying over 600 pounds of gold, 1,038 silver bars, and 250,000 silver coins; the value of the treasure was estimated at four hundred million dollars.

In 1973 Fisher's son Dirk found the ship's anchor and three silver bars in shallow water about seven miles from the ship's actual resting place. Because of its location, Dirk's find proved to be misleading for the search party; the "false find" cost Fisher several years. More importantly, it was also tragic: Dirk continued to search in the same treacherous waters, and two years later his boat capsized, killing him and his wife.

The search for the *Atocha* cost Fisher a great deal of money, many years, and even his son's life. However, his efforts were finally rewarded on July 20, 1985. During a routine search, divers found the *Atocha.* Kane, Mel Fisher's younger son, jubilantly radioed the news to his father in Key West. The *Atocha* has since proved to be the most lucrative oceanic find to date. Although this story deals with monetary treasures, the believer should find an important lesson in this account. We should make a diligent effort to seek the lost who are in bondage to sin; they are of inestimable value to God.

A. W. Tozer, a pastor and well-known author who is now with the Lord, once wrote, "Men are lost but not abandoned: that is what the Scriptures teach and that is what the church is commissioned to declare." Every Christian is commissioned to carry the gospel of Christ to the unsaved. To meet this responsibility, undaunted by obstacles and abounding with hope, the believer must think biblically about the task. The following are several teachings in the New Testament that emphasize the supreme importance of evangelizing the lost.

Christ came to seek and to save the lost. Jesus clearly revealed the nature of His ministry. He said, "The Son of man is come to save that which was lost" (Matt. 18:11). The Scriptures teach that Christ healed many who were sick, taught His disciples, and by His life and death provided an example for us to follow (cf. I Pet. 2:21). Although every aspect of Christ's earthly ministry was vital, of extreme importance were His redemptive proclamations and work. Even New Testament teaching concerning the incarnation emphasizes Christ's redemptive mission. Paul writes, "But when the fulness of the time was come, God sent forth his Son, made of a woman, made under the law, to redeem them that were under the law, that we might receive the adoption of sons" (Gal. 4:4-5).

Christ's desire to see men rescued from their lost condition is demonstrated by both His mass evangelistic efforts and His many personal evangelistic encounters. (Mark 2:13-17; Luke 19:1-10, 23:32-43; John 1:35-42; and John 4:1-30 are a few examples of Christ's efforts in personal evangelism.) Of course, His message of deliverance from sin was made possible by His death on the cross. The time, effort, and sacrifice that Christ devoted to His evangelistic ministry should compel every Christian to make witnessing a top priority in his life.

Christ commanded His disciples to reach the lost. Christ's design for the ministry of the disciples is most clearly seen in the Great Commission (Matt. 28:18-20; Mark 16:15; Luke 24:46-49). These passages outline several vital truths that underscore the importance of witnessing. First, the Lord Jesus promises His presence and authority to those who witness. Second, believers must spread the gospel throughout the world. Third, the proclamation of the gospel will result in men's identifying with Christ by baptism and becoming known as part of the body of Christ. Finally, instruction about conversion must precede all other teachings concerning Christlikeness.

Christ sent the Holy Spirit to empower believers to reach the lost. In its scope, Acts 1:8 is similar to the Great Commission. Here Christ commands believers to witness in Jerusalem, Judea, Samaria, and the whole world. In other words, Christians today should witness everywhere and at all times. In order to help the Christian meet this responsibility, the Holy Spirit indwells the believer. The Spirit of God leads the Christian (Rom. 8:14) and strengthens him (Eph. 3:16) for the task of proclaiming the truth with boldness.

Christ expects us to witness as part of our worship of Him. How better can the Christian honor Christ and show his confidence in the Lord's power to save than by witnessing to others? Certainly the apostle Paul understood this principle and viewed his efforts in winning the lost as an offering that he presented to the Lord. He says, "That I should be the minister of Jesus Christ to the Gentiles, ministering the gospel of God, that the offering up of the Gentiles might be acceptable, being sanctified by the Holy Ghost" (Rom. 15:16).

Christ views witnessing as evidence of the genuineness of our salvation. Jesus says, "Whosoever therefore shall confess me before men, him will I confess also before my Father which is in heaven. But whosoever shall deny me before men, him will I also deny before my Father which is in heaven" (Matt. 10:32-33). Romans 10:10-11 reiterates this teaching: "For with the heart man believeth unto righteousness; and with the mouth confession is made unto salvation. For the scripture saith, Whosoever believeth on him shall not be ashamed." If a person is truly saved, he will testify of Christ's saving power that he has personally experienced.

Why Witnessing Is Important

1. Christ came to seek and to save the lost.
2. Christ commanded His disciples to reach the lost.
3. Christ sent the Holy Spirit to empower believers to reach the lost.
4. Christ expects us to witness as part of our worship to Him.
5. Christ views witnessing as evidence of the genuineness of our salvation.

II. Various Responses to Witnessing (Matt. 13)

Our Lord taught that not everyone who hears the gospel will respond with saving faith. The parable of the sower (or more appropriately, the parable of the soils) teaches this truth. Christ related the parable in Matthew 13:3-9 and explained it in verses 18-23. The reader must not conclude from the three types of poor soil that seventy-five percent of the people to whom he witnesses will not respond favorably. Christ did not intend the parable to reflect the actual percentage of positive and negative responses. Rather, Christ emphasized that the believer can expect varying responses to his evangelistic efforts. In reality, even the positive and negative responses will vary.

The Hard-Hearted Hearer (v. 19) The hard soil in verse 19 is described as "the way side." This word refers to a well-worn path beside a plowed field. Some of the seed that the sower scatters falls on the path but does not penetrate the hard ground. When confronted with the Word, some people, like hardened paths, do not let the message penetrate their hearts. Someone may not receive the gospel because he does not understand the message  (v. 19). This tragedy should not be the result of an unclear presentation; rather, it should happen only because the hearer refuses to understand or accept the truth.

The Impulsive Hearer (vv. 20-21) Verses 20 and 21 mention the emotional or impulsive response. This type of ground is described as "stony"; in other words, there is a thick slab of limestone inches below the surface which does not permit roots to go deep enough to obtain water and nutrients. Therefore, when the sun is hot, the warm soil incubates the seed and causes quick growth but eventually scorches the plant because the roots cannot get water. The heat of the sun is analogous to persecution, and the quick growth to a thoughtless, emotional, or impulsive response. If a person does not consider the cost before trusting Christ, he will not stand firm when hard times come. Obviously, this description refers to a person who has made a hasty, emotional decision but who does not demonstrate true, saving faith in Christ.

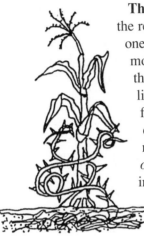

The Unproductive Hearer (v. 22) Of all the responses to the seed of the Word, the one represented by thorny ground is the most difficult to explain. This soil receives the seed, and there appears to be some life; yet sinful influences keep the plant from bearing any fruit. The meaning becomes clear, however, when one recognizes that Jesus is speaking of *observable* responses to the gospel. It is impossible to determine the spiritual condition of this type of person, but this ambiguity is precisely the point of Christ's teaching. Some seem to profess Christ genuinely, but they bear no fruit. It is difficult to tell whether they are carnal Christians (I Cor. 3:1-2) or lost men (Matt. 7:15-20). Scripture teaches that at times there is simply no way to know the true heart condition of people (Matt. 13:24-30).

The Genuine Hearer (v. 23) The last kind of soil is "good ground." Sowing upon this type of ground results in growth and fruit. The quantity of fruit may vary, but the harvest is abundant. This soil describes the person who receives the incorruptible seed of the Word and is born again (I Pet. 1:23). He receives the Word, obeys it, and begins to bear fruit.

III. The Right Attitude for Witnessing (Luke 15)

The longest New Testament passage that concerns reaching the lost is Luke 15. This thirty-two-verse chapter contains Christ's most concentrated instruction on the subject. Here Jesus responds to the objection of outwardly pious religionists to His efforts to reach the lost, and He gives positive instruction to believers concerning how to approach the lost.

The passage contains three parables about lost items: the lost sheep (vv. 4-7), the lost coin (vv. 8-10), and the lost son, commonly called the prodigal son (vv. 11-32). In each parable, the lost item represents a person who is lost in sin. In each case, the lost item or person is found. These parables emphasize two necessary characteristics for reaching the lost.

Be aggressive. Three vital qualities characterize this aggressiveness in reaching the lost. First, *persistence* marks aggressive witnessing. The shepherd sought until he found the lost sheep (v. 4). The woman searched her house, sweeping every corner, until she found her missing coin (v. 8). Although the father never left his estate to search for his son, the passage implies that he eagerly anticipated his son's return ("when he was yet a great way off, his father saw him"—v. 20).

Preoccupation with the lost is a second characteristic of aggressive witnessing. Although the shepherd had ninety-nine remaining sheep, he was intensely concerned about the lost one (v. 4). The woman still possessed nine coins, but she naturally wanted to find the one she had lost (v. 8). The father had one remaining son and a great estate, but he never lost his intense desire for his lost son to return (v. 20).

Third, this aggressiveness is tempered by *compassion*. When the shepherd found the sheep, he carried it on his shoulders back to the fold (v. 5). When the father saw his son from a great distance, he had compassion on him (v. 20).

Aggressiveness is necessary for the effective soulwinner, for the lost generally do not seek the Lord. They are usually satisfied with their way of life and usually do not worry about their fate. The believer is responsible to seek these lost people, warn them of the consequences of their sin, and lead them to Christ, the true Shepherd.

Be optimistic. Not everyone who hears the gospel will accept the Lord, but many will. Although the parable of the sower emphasizes the variety of responses, Christ's three parables of the lost things do not share this emphasis. These parables highlight the *finding* of the lost item, as well as the consequent rejoicing. The fact that every lost item is found is a cause for optimism.

In addition, the parables consistently note the *rejoicing* that takes place after the lost item or person is found. The repentant sinner brings joy to the heart of God (v. 7). When the ungodly turn to the Lord, the angels rejoice (v. 10). The household of faith engages in joyful celebration when a lost one comes to Christ (vv. 22-24, 32). These responses should encourage the believer in his evangelistic efforts.

Another encouraging aspect of these parables is that the believer's responsibility in evangelism is *reasonable*. Jesus twice stated that the heavens rejoice over even one sinner who repents (vv. 7, 10). God does not set unreasonable or impossible goals for the believer. A Christian should not be discouraged by the sheer number of lost people; by God's grace he should seek to win one person at a time.

IV. God's Part in Witnessing

Personal evangelism is a divine/human endeavor. Only God can deliver a man from the consequences of sin, yet God has decided to use His servants to reach lost men. However, the believer's evangelistic efforts will not be successful if he does not rely upon the power of God. Salvation is a supernatural event in the life of a sinful man; no amount of human effort alone can save a lost man.

God answers prayer. Obedient Christians see their prayers answered (John 15:7). If a man prays for the salvation of others, he is clearly praying for the will of God (II Pet. 3:9). If an obedient Christian prays for the salvation of a lost person, he can confidently expect that man's eventual conversion (Matt. 7:7).

In addition to praying for the conversion of the lost, the soul-winner should pray for himself and the evangelistic efforts of others. Paul asked the Ephesians to pray that he would proclaim the gospel boldly (Eph. 6:18-20). He urged the Colossians to pray that he would have opportunities to witness (Col. 4:2-3). He also asked the Thessalonians to pray for the spread of the gospel through him and for protection from those who would oppose it (II Thess. 3:1-2). The Lord Jesus exhorts us to pray for Him to burden the hearts of Christians to become faithful witnesses because the fields are ready for the harvest (Matt. 9:37-38).

God works through His Spirit. The lost are in a desperate condition; their minds are utterly darkened to the gospel (II Cor. 4:4). They cannot receive spiritual truth (I Cor. 2:14). They are unable to help themselves out of their spiritual death (Eph. 2:1), and by themselves they can demonstrate no desire toward the things of God (John 6:44). Only the Holy Spirit's work in the heart of a sinner can draw a man to Christ.

As the gospel is preached, the Spirit of God works mightily in the heart of the lost man. He convicts him of the sin of unbelief and convinces him of the true nature of Christ and the certainty of judgment (John 16:8-11). He enlightens his mind to the truth (John 1:9; Acts 26:18; Eph. 1:18; Heb. 6:4-9) and draws him to Christ (John 12:32). God will not force a man to be saved, but no one can blame God if a man rejects the truth and goes to hell. God works through His Spirit to help lost men gain life through Christ.

God works through you. As a Christian, you may wonder why God did not take you home to heaven immediately after you were saved. The answer may be found in Christ's high-priestly prayer in John 17. The Lord prayed on behalf of believers, "I pray not that thou shouldest take them out of the world, but that thou shouldest keep them from the evil. They are not of the world, even as I am not of the world. Sanctify them through thy truth: thy word is truth. As thou hast sent me into the world, even so have I also sent them into the world" (vv. 15-18). We would be able to praise and fellowship with God more effectively in heaven; however, there are no lost souls in heaven. God has left believers in this world in order to reach lost souls for Him. Witnessing to others is an important aspect of our service to Christ.

Review Questions

1. What single word in the following verse indicates the Christian's relationship to lost people?

   "Now then we are ambassadors for Christ, as though God did beseech you by us: we pray you in Christ's stead, be ye reconciled to God" (II Cor. 5:20).

2. Why did you pick that word?

3. Why is Matthew 13:3-9 more appropriately called the Parable of the Soils than the Parable of the Sower?

4. List five works the Spirit of God performs in the heart of a lost man.

____5. God uses humans as witnesses because He speaks to
        sinners only through a mediator.

____6. Praying for specific people to be saved is unnecessary
        because God wants everyone to be saved.

Which option in each of the following two sets is not one
of the "teachings in the New Testament that emphasize the
supreme importance of evangelizing the lost"?

____ 7.

    A. Christ told us to witness.
    B. Christ expects us to witness.
    C. Our witnessing shows we are really saved.
    D. Christ promised us many people would believe the
       gospel.

____ 8.

    A. Witnessing shows we are not ashamed of Christ.
    B. Christ never turns away sinners we bring to Him.
    C. Christ gave us the Holy Spirit to help us.
    D. Christ witnessed to lost people.

After each paragraph below identify which type of soil
most likely represents the person described. Explain why you
chose each answer.

You met a guy named Leopold on visitation. After hearing
the gospel from you, he tearfully repented of his sin and
prayed to accept Christ. He started coming to your church
that week. He would show up at the youth meetings, always
acting like he was having a good time. But he came only once

the following month, and then stopped coming. You went to visit him at home, but he seemed distracted. He said he has been too busy lately to come to church but promised to come again soon. After three months, he still has not come back.

_____9. Leopold appears to be

    A. the way side.
    B. stony ground.
    C. thorny ground.
    D. good ground.

    Explain:

You have been friends with Juanita since she joined your church over a year ago. Halfway through your senior year, Juanita became a little depressed about her family's financial situation and started diligently researching which college major brought the highest starting salary. She went to a different college than you did, and now you rarely hear from her. You found out that she is not going to any church in her college town and that she started dating an older student who doesn't seem to be a Christian.

_____10. Juanita appears to be

    A. the way side.
    B. stony ground.
    C. thorny ground.
    D. good ground.

    Explain:

CHAPTER THREE

Following a Plan for Witnessing

③

Memory Verses: Luke 24:45-48

A Christian will witness clearly and thoroughly when he follows a plan. Paul exhorts, "Let all things be done decently and in order" (I Cor. 14:40). A cogent presentation is important because saving faith is based on a clear understanding of the gospel (cf. Rom. 10:17). A person must know to what or whom he is entrusting his eternal welfare. If he does not understand upon whom he is relying for salvation, then he has been misled. A misplaced or misled faith is not true saving faith.

Each witnessing opportunity brings the challenge of adapting to the particular needs of a lost person. The soulwinner must answer his questions and address his particular concerns and circumstances. Yet no matter how much the believer has to adapt his presentation, he must be sure to present the gospel clearly. Mapping out a plan for witnessing will facilitate this goal.

Maps are vital aids for finding the way to any destination. Cartography, the science of mapmaking, has been practiced since before the birth of Christ. Babylonian maps recorded on clay tablets date back to 2300 B.C. Anaximander, a Greek mathematician, produced a map of the world around 550 B.C. Ptolemy of Alexandria (A.D. 90-168) published an eight-volume work entitled *Guide to Geography,* a resource which greatly influenced mapmaking for nearly a thousand years. Martin Waldseemuller's world map produced in 1507 was probably the first to include America. Cartography became especially important during the age of exploration, for "a newly discovered

I appreciate your uncle's attempt to draw us a map, but Ptolemy of Alexandria he's not.

place can only be systematically reached again if it has been mapped" *(Encyclopedia Americana,* 18:287).

In the spiritual realm, lost men cannot find the way to Christ without proper directions. Christians have been entrusted with the gospel and should be able to point others to Christ. A poorly drawn map causes confusion and does not provide much help in reaching a destination. In the same way, the believer must be able to present clearly the plan of salvation. The rest of this chapter provides a workable step-by-step plan for pointing others to Christ.

I. Initiate the Conversation.

The soulwinner labors for men's souls. He is a farmer who sows the seed of the Word, waters it, and reaps the spiritual harvest. He is a soldier warring against Satan, who deceives men by darkening their minds. He is an athlete striving for the victory in the race against the powers of sin, the world, and the Devil in the lives of others. These metaphors suggest that the Christian is on the offensive. The believer does not simply provide a passive, "silent" witness; he actively seeks to reach others with the gospel of Christ.

Because the New Testament regularly portrays the believer as the aggressor in the search for souls; therefore, he should seek out opportunities and, to the best of his ability, even *create* opportunities to witness for Christ. An unsaved person normally does not seek the gospel, nor does he usually initiate a conversation about spiritual matters. The believer, therefore, is responsible for presenting the gospel to others.

Build rapport. The believer can witness to someone most effectively when there is a reasonable amount of mutual trust and emotional affinity. This relationship is called *rapport* [ra•PORE]. A believer may gain rapport with someone through a previous acquaintance, common interests, or friendship. Paul understood the importance of gaining rapport with his audience. When he preached to the Athenians on Mars Hill (Acts 17:18-34), he referred to their altar erected to the "UNKNOWN GOD." Paul stated that he knew this God, and he then began to preach about Him (v. 23). The apostle also struck a common chord with the Athenians by quoting some of their poets (v. 28). It is not always easy to find common ground with someone, but it is very important in gaining an opportunity to share the gospel.

Paul also sought to build rapport with fellow Jews. He identified himself as a kinsman, and he attended the synagogue, participating in the services. He also used the Old Testament, the Jewish Scriptures, to present Christ.

Although Paul usually preached to total strangers, he tried to identify with them as much as time and circumstances allowed. He outlined his practice in I Corinthians 9:22: "I am made all things to all men, that I might by all means save some." Paul's ability to gain rapport with others usually earned him an opportunity to present Christ.

Stimulate interest. After the soulwinner builds rapport with someone, he should then look for the right moment to turn the conversation toward spiritual matters. The soulwinner may accomplish this by asking certain questions. The following questions may be used to direct the conversation toward Christ.

"Has anyone ever shown you from the Bible how to have your sins forgiven? May I show you some brief passages from the Bible that teach this truth?"

"Our church teaches the Bible. May I take a few minutes to show you what the primary lesson of the Bible is?"

"Most people have thought about God at some point in their lives. May I show you what the Bible teaches about knowing God in this life and in the afterlife?"

"The most important command in the Bible is to love God. May I take a few moments to show you how a person can love God according to the Bible?"

"If you were to stand before God today, do you know what you would say to gain entrance to heaven? May I show you what the Bible teaches about going to heaven?"

"Do you know what it is that God says should be the greatest influence in all of life's decisions? May I show you from Scripture what that influence is?"

"Almost everyone is interested in having a life full of peace and satisfaction. Would you be willing to let me share with you how you can obtain peace and joy from the God of the Bible?"

Obviously, the soulwinner can use other questions, but these questions demonstrate that there are many ways to turn a conversation tactfully to a presentation of the gospel. The soulwinner should ask questions that are appropriate in the context of the conversation. Also, he should make an effort to make the lost person feel at ease even if he cannot answer the question.

II. Follow an Outline.

Saving faith is based on certain basic truths of the Bible. The presentation of these truths, therefore, must be clear and complete. One way to insure that the gospel is presented clearly and completely is to use an outline. The soulwinner may follow this outline rigidly, or he may adapt it according to the particular circumstances or needs of the hearer. The following outline also provides transitional statements to allow for a smooth and logical progression between main points.

Who is God?

He is a loving Savior.

The Bible teaches in I John 4:8 and 16 that God's very nature is love. He is controlled by a willingness to sacrifice Himself for the spiritual good of man. The Scriptures also teach in John 3:16 that God's love is extended to all men through the sacrificial death of His Son, Jesus Christ. Second Corinthians 13:11 states that those who trust Christ as Savior will have the God of love dwelling with them.

He is a just judge.

No one respects a judge who hands down sentences that contradict the law. Naturally, men would lose all respect for God if He did not remain fair by rewarding good and punishing evil. Psalm 75:7 teaches that God is the judge of all men. He will always judge accurately and fairly, as Genesis 18:25 and Psalm 96:10 teach. Hebrews 9:27 says that "it is appointed unto men once to die, but after this the judgment." After a man dies, he becomes subject to judgment.

He is Lord over all.

God created all things and therefore owns all things. That ownership gives Him the right to control all things and expect His creatures to submit to Him. Colossians 1:16 says, "For by him were all things created, that are in heaven, and that are in earth, visible and invisible, whether they be thrones, or dominions, or principalities, or powers: all things were created by him, and for him."

For a man to ignore or rebel against God is a sin that will bring eternal consequences. Paul warns, "Nay but, O man, who art thou that repliest against God? Shall the thing formed say to him that formed it, Why hast thou made me thus? Hath not the potter power over the clay, of the same lump to make one vessel unto honour, and another unto dishonour?" (Rom. 9:20-21). Christ is Lord over all; He deserves our loyalty and obedience.

Transition: God loves man and wants to show him kindness, but He is just and cannot overlook man's sin.

What is man's problem?

Man is guilty because of his sin nature.

Every man is bound to sin because he has sin in his heart. Men are born this way. Just as a dog acts like a dog, a pig behaves like a pig, and a snake writhes and strikes like a snake, so man acts like a sinner because it is in his nature to sin. Psalm 51:5 and Romans 5:12 teach this truth.

Man is guilty because of his sinful acts.

Man is condemned by God not only because he has a sinful nature but also because he has performed sinful deeds. Every man has entertained sinful thoughts and committed acts that make him worthy of condemnation. Romans 3:23 says, "For all have sinned, and come short of the glory of God."

Man is separated from God because of sin.

According to Habakkuk 1:13, God abhors the sight of evil. Sin causes a great separation between God and man. Isaiah taught, "But your iniquities have separated between you and your God, and your sins have hid his face from you, that he will not hear" (59:2). By sinning, man has earned spiritual death (separation from God) and physical death for himself. Romans 6:23 speaks of the consequences of man's sin.

Transition: How can a man solve his problem of sin? He must come to Christ, who conquered sin on the cross.

What has God done?

Christ has become the God-man.

Jesus Christ is God; yet He came to earth in human flesh. This is the meaning of the apostle John's words, "The Word [Christ] was made flesh, and dwelt among us" (John 1:14). Christ was the fulfillment of Isaiah's prophecy recorded in Matthew 1:23, "Behold, a virgin shall be with child, and shall bring forth a son, and they shall call his name Emmanuel, which being interpreted is, God with us." As God, Christ possessed all the eternal power and purity of God. He alone could accomplish the miracle of salvation for man.

Christ has lived a perfect life.

Had Christ been a sinner like other men, He could not have died for the sins of mankind. The New Testament clearly teaches that no one can legitimately accuse Christ of having committed a sin (II Cor. 5:21). He was tempted in every way possible, but He never yielded to temptation (Heb. 4:15).

Christ bore our sins and their penalty on the cross.

The apostle Peter wrote that Christ bore our sins while He hung on the cross (I Pet. 2:21-24). He suffered there for us so that we would not have to experience the wrath of God in hell forever. He was our propitiation; in other words, He bore God's wrath in our stead (I John 2:1-2).

Christ rose from the grave as proof of His victory over sin and death.

The resurrection of Christ is part of the good news of salvation (I Cor. 15:4). Speaking of the Lord Jesus, Paul wrote, "Who was delivered for our offences, and was raised again for our justification" (Rom. 4:25). The resurrection of Christ was part of the great saving act of God on behalf of sinful men.

Because Christ rose from the dead, the believer has the promise that one day his body will be resurrected and that he will live forever in the presence of God (I Cor. 15:54-57). This is the greatest of all benefits of faith in Christ.

Transition: Christ has borne sin and its penalty for all men. However, men are not automatically free from their sins. The work of Christ on the cross is effective only for those who personally accept Christ as Lord and Savior.

What must man do?

Man must turn from his sin.

Turning from the control and love of sin at conversion is called repentance. **Repentance** involves both turning from the controlling influence of sin and turning to God (I Thess. 1:9-10).

Man must place his confidence in Christ.

Saving faith is not merely the *knowledge* that Jesus is the Savior and Lord of all; even the demons *understand* certain truths about God (James 2:19). True faith is a careful, thorough decision to trust what Christ did on the cross and what He teaches in the Bible (Luke 14:27-33).

The one who believes in Christ decides to rely on Christ as his Savior from the penalty and power of sin. He also places his faith in God to guide and control his life. True faith results in salvation from sin. Acts 16:31 states, "Believe on the Lord Jesus Christ, and thou shalt be saved."

III. Conclude with an Invitation.

Ask the lost person if he understands your presentation. As the believer presents the gospel to a lost person, the Holy Spirit will begin to work in the sinner's heart and mind. Second Corinthians 4:6 says, "For God, who commanded the light to shine out of darkness, hath shined in our hearts, to give the light of the knowledge of the glory of God in the face of Jesus Christ." Few things in life are as amazing to behold as the Lord's enlightening the mind of an unbeliever and making him receptive to the gospel. A scriptural example of the Holy Spirit's working is Lydia of Thyatira, who was converted to Christ while visiting Philippi. Luke recounts this incident in Acts 16:14, "And a certain woman named Lydia, a seller of purple, of the city of Thyatira, which worshipped God, heard us: whose heart the Lord opened, that she attended unto the things which were spoken of Paul."

The Scriptures clearly teach that God is at work in the mind of an unbeliever while the truth is being presented. However, this fact does not lessen the believer's responsibility to present the truth in a clear and interesting way. Colossians 4:6 exhorts, "Let your speech be alway with grace, seasoned with salt, that ye may know how ye ought to answer every man."

In addition to presenting the message clearly, the soulwinner should make sure that the hearer has understood the presentation. Remember that one of Satan's devices to keep men in the bondage of sin is confusion about the truth. Jesus taught in Matthew 13:19, "When any one heareth the word of the kingdom, and understandeth it not, then cometh the wicked one, and catcheth away that which was sown in his heart." The soulwinner must remember that "God is not the author of confusion, but of peace, as in all churches of the saints" (I Cor. 14:33). **Encourage an immediate decision for Christ.** Peter wrote, "The Lord is not slack concerning his promise, as some men count slackness; but is longsuffering to usward, not willing that any should perish, but that all should come to repentance" (II Pet. 3:9). God wants the unsaved person to turn from sin and trust in Christ. In the mind of God, now is the best time for a person to be saved. Second Corinthians 6:2 says, "For he saith, I have heard thee in a time accepted, and in the day of salvation have I succoured thee: behold, now is the accepted time; behold, now is the day of salvation."

The soulwinner may want to ask the lost person one of the following questions to bring him to a point of salvation.

"Would you like to pray now and receive the gift of eternal life through faith in Christ?"

"Since you understand the good news about Christ and His salvation, would you like to accept Him now as your Savior from sin?"

"Would you like to decide now to become a follower of Christ by trusting in His death and resurrection for you?"

The believer must be cautious about his use of logic and persuasion at this point. He is encouraging the lost person to make the most important decision of his life. A relationship with Christ must not be entered into lightly, and the unsaved person must realize the seriousness of his choice. He must make his choice willingly, not because he is coerced. The soulwinner can always rest in the truth of I Corinthians 3:6: "I have planted, Apollos watered; but God gave the increase." The Christian witness should never stoop to desperate, carnal techniques to pressure someone into making a decision for Christ.

Offer an opportunity to call on the Lord for salvation. A person does not receive salvation simply by repeating a prayer. Salvation is a choice to trust Christ as Savior and Lord for the rest of one's life. This choice occurs in the heart or inner man. However, the Scriptures teach that out of the fullness of the heart the mouth speaks (Matt. 12:34), and prayer is an appropriate expression of the heart. This association is so close that the Scriptures seem to link calling on the Lord with salvation itself. Romans 10:12-13 states, "For the same Lord over all is rich unto all that call upon him. For whosoever shall call upon the name of the Lord shall be saved."

It is a good practice to encourage the lost person to pray aloud rather than silently; articulating one's thoughts often gives more meaning and clarity to them. This prayer should include a statement of trust in Christ as Savior and a statement of allegiance to follow Christ as God, rejecting sin and self as the rulers of life.

Conclusion

As you establish your priorities in life, consider the words of Dr. C. I. Scofield, a man of great missionary fervor and soulwinning zeal, and the editor of America's most loved study Bible, the Scofield Reference Bible.

"Let us leave the government of the world till the King comes. Let us leave the civilizing of the world to be an incidental effect of the presence there of the gospel of Christ. Let us give our time, our strength, our money, our days to make Christ known to every creature" (*Knight's Illustrations for Today*, p. 318).

This statement should express the sentiment of every Christian heart. There are other important priorities in the Christian life, but nothing is more crucial than proclaiming the gospel to the lost in a clear, interesting, and persuasive manner.

Review Questions

_____1. Which verse most clearly shows the importance of building rapport?

    A. I Corinthians 14:40

    B. Romans 10:17

    C. Acts 17:18

    D. I Corinthians 9:22

_____2. Imagine that you just finished witnessing to a person, but he is reluctant to pray to the Lord for salvation at that moment. Which of these represents a proper response?

    A. "That's fine, you can get saved any time you want under any circumstances. Don't hurry."

    B. "I don't want to push you into anything, but please remember that the Bible says in II Corinthians 6:2, 'Now is the accepted time, behold now is the day of salvation.'"

    C. "Come on, you pagan, you need to do it NOW!"

    D. "Why don't you understand? It should be obvious that the plain facts of the case demand that you get saved now."

Imagine that you ask a person whether he understands what you have just presented to him and he responds with one of the statements in the next three questions. In the blank beside each question, write "T" if the statement reflects a proper understanding of the gospel and "F" if it indicates a misconception.

_____3. "What you are saying is I have to switch over to your church if I want to get saved?"

_____4. "What you are saying is I have to ask Jesus to forgive all my sins all at once and to make me a Christian?"

_____5. "What you are saying is I have to love Jesus to get to heaven?"

Short/Long Answer

For the next four sentences, consult the sample outline for witnessing. Give the main point and subpoint along with the Scripture reference that would be the right thing to say next if the person to whom you are witnessing were to say the following:

6. "Do you think God sends people to hell? I just don't see how a loving God could send people to hell!"

7. "I'm not perfect, of course, but I don't really do anything bad."

8. "I know Jesus is a great teacher, and I think it is terrible He was killed, but what does He have to do with me?"

9. "You'll want me to give up drugs if I get saved, right?"

10. From the principles you learned in this chapter, explain why
    questions are appropriate for turning a conversation toward
    spiritual matters.

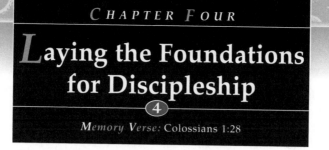

In this chapter, we begin the study of the second part of disciple making, personal discipleship. After you lead someone to trust Christ, you start teaching him the things a Christian must know. You may also meet someone who, although he has been saved for a while, never had this basic instruction. Even though you did not lead him to Christ, you have the privilege of personally teaching him the basics of the Christian faith.

On the other hand, you may want to set up a Bible study with someone who is not saved in order to lead him to Christ. Some people who do not trust Christ on first hearing the gospel still want to learn more. Like Nicodemus, they want time to study the Bible and think through it for themselves. Leading such a person through a self-study course is a great way to deal with questions systematically and to provide a summary of what the Bible teaches.

To gain a new skill, you have to practice it. We are going to practice the skill of discipleship in two ways: first, by putting you in the role of a new Christian taking a basic course; second, by allowing you to lead another Christian through the same course. By first being the learner, you can work on mastering the material you will later teach. By practicing being the teacher, you will get an idea of what it will be like to hold someone accountable for the lessons, summarize the basics of Christianity in your own words, and answer another person's questions.

This chapter contains the first five lessons in James Berg's discipleship manual *Basics for Believers*. A separate copy of the booklet is included with this course for you to use to practice discipling another Christian. It covers the basics of Christianity in a simple but thorough fashion. Work through the lessons, filling in all the blanks with the most accurate answers you can devise. Remember that you will need to be able to clearly explain each answer to another person.

Introduction

Unfortunately, many people have looked upon Christianity as just another religion. Were it not for one basic difference, this might be true. Genuine Christianity is not a religion; it is a relationship. It is a relationship with Jesus Christ.

No one becomes a Christian by joining a church or being baptized or confirmed. One must personally know Jesus Christ (by experience) to be a Christian.

There is only one way to know Christ personally—by knowing and believing what God has told us about Him in God's Word, the Bible. In the Bible, God spells out the conditions that must be met before He accepts anyone into His family. It also tells us how to build our relationship with Him once we have become children of God.

If you are not a Christian or do not know whether you are, these simple Bible studies are for you. If you are a new Christian, these studies will help you to build your relationship with God. All you will need is some time alone, a pen or pencil, and a Bible. It is suggested that you use the Authorized Version of the Bible (the King James Version) to answer the questions. Read each verse carefully and prayerfully. Then answer the questions in your own words.

God says that the most important thing in the world is that you know Him personally. Listen to what He says in Jeremiah 9:23-24:

"Thus saith the Lord, Let not the wise man glory in his wisdom, neither let the mighty man glory in his might, let not the rich man glory in his riches: But let him that glorieth glory in this, that *he understandeth and knoweth me*" (emphasis added).

These studies can help you to "understand and know" the God of heaven.

Eternal Life—Accepting God's Gift

People today are constantly making big promises. Television advertisements promise everything from cleaner dishes to smoother-riding cars. All of these promises are trivial, however, when compared to the promise of eternal life that God offers to man.

It is sad that not every man has this eternal life. God's Word says that there are two groups of people in this world.

1. According to I John 5:11-12, what are these two groups?

    a.

    b.

2. What determines whether a person has eternal life
    (I John 5:12)?

3. The Bible says that all men are sinners. In Romans 3:23 God declares that "all have sinned, and come short of the glory of God." Every man has broken God's law and deserves God's punishment. The Bible says that "the wages of sin is death" (Rom. 6:23). Even though man deserves to be punished for his sin, what did God do (John 3:16)?

4. Can a person do anything on his own to have eternal life (Titus 3:5)?

5. What must a person do to become part of God's family and have eternal life (John 1:12)?

6. If a person truly desires to receive Christ and have eternal life, what will be his attitude toward sin (Isa. 55:7a)?

Note: A person who genuinely wants to be saved will express an attitude of repentance toward his sin. This means that he will not only acknowledge his sin (confess it to God), but also he will be sorry enough about it that he will turn away from it.

7. What does God say about a person who has not received Christ and repented of his sin (John 3:18)?

8. Is it possible for a person to know whether he has eternal life? (I John 5:13)

9. Can you personally say, without hesitation, that you have God's gift of eternal life?

10. If you answered yes to question 9 above, what reason(s) can you give for your answer?

For additional study about accepting God's gift of eternal life, see John 3:1-21.

Assurance–Believing God's Promises

Once a person repents of his sin and accepts God's gift of eternal life, Satan will begin to intimidate him and will try to cast doubts in his mind. This can be expected since Jesus called Satan the "father" of lies (John 8:44). Read the following promises carefully and note what God has said He will do when a person asks Christ to save him.

"He that believeth on the Son hath everlasting life: and he that believeth not the Son shall not see life; but the wrath of God abideth on him" (John 3:36).

"And I give unto them eternal life; and they shall never perish, neither shall any man pluck them out of my hand" (John 10:28).

"Him that cometh to me I will in no wise cast out" (John 6:37*b*).

1. A lack of assurance can be an indication that you are not trusting God's promises. Have you ever repented of your sin and asked God to save you?

   Is it possible for God to lie or go back on a promise (Titus 1:2)?

   If God cannot lie and you have asked Christ to save you, what does John 5:24 say about you?

2. A lack of assurance can also mean that there is sin in your life that you have not confessed to God. It stands between you and God. What does Proverbs 28:13 say about the man who harbors sin in his life?

   If you have truly trusted Christ, you will forsake your sin; but should you sin, it is not necessary that you be saved again. You are already a member of God's family. He does not throw you out of the family, but He is disappointed and grieved over your sin. What does I John 1:9 say you are to do when you sin?

   What does this verse say that God will do?

   After you are saved, you begin to receive greater assurance as you see certain evidences in your life. Look up these verses below and note the evidences they describe.

1. Romans 8:16–The Holy Spirit bears witness to my spirit. The Holy Spirit assures you,

2. I John 4:19–You find that you love

3. I John 3:14–You find that you love

4. John 14:27–God gives you

5. According to II Corinthians 5:17, what should be happening to your old desires and ways?

6. Galatians 5:17–What is going on inside you now?

Each of these evidences indicates that you are God's child. They will grow as you feed daily on God's Word. To help you resist the doubts that Satan will send your way, memorize the verses on assurance from the "Memory Verses" page in the Additional Helps for Christian Growth section in the back of this book.

If after you have studied this chapter you still do not have a real assurance of your salvation, read and reread I John 5:11-13. Then study through the first chapter of this book again and seek the help of another believer who is sure that he is saved. God desires that you feel secure in His family.

God's Word–Listening to God Speak

The Bible is a revelation of God's instructions to man. Since God Himself is the author, His Word possesses absolute authority over man. It touches on every area of life. Jesus said, "Man shall not live by bread alone, but by every word that proceedeth out of the mouth of God" (Matt. 4:4).

There are countless benefits to be gained from reading and studying God's Word.

1. *It is the source of the believer's faith.*

   "Faith cometh by hearing, and hearing by the word of God" (Rom. 10:17).

2. *It cleanses us as we obey it.*

   "Now ye are clean through the word which I have spoken unto you" (John 15:3).

"Wherewithal shall a young man cleanse his way? by taking heed thereto according to thy word" (Ps. 119:9).

3. *It gives us direction and understanding.*

"Thy word is a lamp unto my feet, and a light unto my path" (Ps. 119:105).

"The entrance of thy words giveth light; it giveth understanding to the simple" (Ps. 119:130).

4. *It gives victory over Satan when we apply it.*

"Thy word have I hid in mine heart, that I might not sin against thee" (Ps. 119:11).

Many other things can be said about the Bible. Read the following questions and look up the answers in your Bible.

1. The Bible was written over a period of sixteen centuries by some forty men, yet all sixty-six books bear a remarkable unity. They teach the same salvation and the same moral standards, and they all point to the same Savior. Who guided the writers so that they all agree (II Pet. 1:21)?

   Note: This divine guidance of what the writers recorded is called *inspiration.*

2. What two statements about the Bible are given in II Timothy 3:16?

   a.
   b.

3. What must we do to make the Bible personally beneficial (II Tim. 2:15)?

4. What should be our attitude toward the Bible (Ps. 119:97)?

5. Job considered God's Word to be the most important thing in his life. How do we know this (Job 23:12*b*)?

6. Why is it so important for new Christians to begin reading and studying the Bible right away (I Pet. 2:2)?

For additional study about listening to God speak, see Luke 8:4-15. Read through "A Plan for a Daily Quiet Time with God" in the Additional Helps for Christian Growth section. This will give you some help in setting up a daily time of Bible reading and application for your life.

*T*emptation–Resisting God's Enemy

A recently saved Indian chief was asked by a missionary how things were going in his new faith. The chief replied that he felt as if two dogs were fighting inside. The black dog wanted him to do evil, and the white dog wanted him to do right. When asked by the missionary which dog was winning, the chief replied, "The dog I feed the most."

The apostle Paul wrote of this same struggle when he said, "the flesh lusteth [sets its desires] against the Spirit, and the Spirit against the flesh: and these are contrary the one to the other: so that ye cannot do the things that ye would" (Gal. 5:17).

After a person becomes a Christian, he finds that God's Spirit is continually prompting him to do right. At the same time, Satan, God's enemy, tries harder to tempt the believer to sin. Thus a continual and fierce battle rages. God's plan for over-coming Satan is set forth in the Bible. Study the follow-ing passages carefully to learn how to resist Satan.

1. What description of Satan is given in I Peter 5:8?

Photodisc, Inc.

2. Hebrews 2:14 says that Christ rendered him powerless who "had the power of death, that is, the devil." Since Satan is a defeated enemy, what does God want us to be (Rom. 8:37)?

3. The first battleground for most conflicts is the mind. What is a Christian to do when evil thoughts arise (II Cor. 10:5)?

4. James 4:7 gives a two-fold plan for victory over Satan. List the two elements of this plan.

   a.
   b.

5. How did Jesus "resist the devil" (Matt. 4:4, 7, 10)?

6. What did Jesus tell His disciples to do to resist Satan's temptations (Matt. 26:41)?

7. Besides not allowing you to be tempted past your level of endurance, what does God promise to do for you (I Cor. 10:13)?

8. What "way of escape" is described in II Timothy 2:22a?

9. If you should fail to resist the Devil or fail to take the way of escape and find that you have sinned, what should you do (I John 1:9)?

10. Read Psalm 139:23-24. Take a moment to ask God to examine your heart and mind. List your areas of weakness on the following chart. Find Bible verses from "Verses for Victory" in Additional Helps for Christian Growth or find verses in

other study helps and begin fortifying yourself against Satan's attacks.

Sins and Weaknesses	Verses for Victory

For additional help in resisting God's enemy, study Ephesians 6:10-18.

Prayer–Talking With God

Communication is the basis for *every* relationship. People who do not talk to each other never grow very close together. Reading the Bible and praying are the two basic activities for developing your relationship with God. Just as there are countless benefits from reading and studying God's Word, so there are untold blessings to be reaped through personal contact with God through prayer.

1. *It is the means of getting help in times of need.*

   "Let us therefore come boldly unto the throne of grace, that we may obtain mercy, and find grace to help in time of need" (Heb. 4:16).

2. *It is the means of obtaining forgiveness of sins.*

"If we confess our sins, he is faithful and just to forgive us our sins, and to cleanse us from all unrighteousness" (I John 1:9).

3. *It is the means to spiritual strength.*

"Men ought always to pray, and not to faint" (Luke 18:1*b*).

4. *It makes God more real to the believer.*

"Draw nigh [near] to God, and he will draw nigh to you" (James 4:8*a*).

5. *It brings joy to the believer.*

"In thy presence is fulness of joy" (Ps. 16:11*b*).

6. *It is God's way of providing our needs.*

"Ask, and it shall be given you; seek, and ye shall find; knock, and it shall be opened unto you" (Matt. 7:7).

7. *It is God's cure for worry.*

"Be careful [worried] for nothing; but in every thing by prayer and supplication with thanksgiving let your requests be made known unto God. And the peace of God, which passeth all understanding, shall keep [guard] your hearts and minds through Christ Jesus" (Phil. 4:6-7).

God's Word is full of promises to answer our prayers. However, along with each promise is a certain condition that God wants us to meet. State the conditions described in the verses below.

1. I John 3:22

    a.
    b.

2. John 15:7

    a.
    b.

3. John 14:13

4. Mark 11:24

5. I John 5:14-15

> *Note:* We will know what is "according to His will" as we
> study the Word of God and pray "in the Spirit" (conscious
> of the Holy Spirit's promptings in our hearts). The Holy
> Spirit helps us pray and "maketh intercession for the saints
> according to the will of God" (Rom. 8:26-27).

Sometimes, however, it seems that God does not hear us.
Sometimes He does not answer. In either case there is a reason.
Look up the following references to discover some hindrances to
prayer.

1. James 4:3
2. Isaiah 59:1-2
3. Mark 11:25-26

For additional help about talking with God, see Matthew 6:5-15.

Review Questions

_____1. "An attitude of repentance toward sin" involves only a recognition that sin is very damaging.

_____2. A truly saved person may occasionally doubt his salvation.

_____3. When a new believer needs guidance from God, he should open his Bible randomly and read until a certain verse strikes him as relevant.

_____4. Prayer is necessary to gain forgiveness of sin.

Multiple Choice

_____5. Which of the following is not a legitimate reason for a person to believe he has eternal life?

A. He believes God has mercy on sinners.
B. He wants to go to heaven forever.
C. He received Jesus Christ as his Savior.
D. He knows Jesus died to save him from his sin.

_____6. If a new convert were to tell you that he is doubting his salvation, which of the following would be a valid reason for his doubt?

A. Satan's lies
B. Failure to trust God's promises
C. Unconfessed sin
D. Each of these could be a valid reason for doubt.

7. What is "the first battleground for most conflicts" between Satan and the Spirit of God?

8. What member of the Trinity actually helps us pray?

9. What is the basis for every relationship?

10. Suppose you reach the lesson on temptation with a disciple. He tells you that, though he believes drunkenness is sin, he is having terrible problems fighting the temptation to drink liquor. List three verses used in that lesson and write how you would apply each one to this tempted Christian's situation.

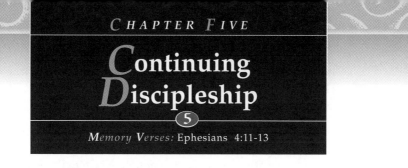

CHAPTER FIVE

Continuing Discipleship

⑤

Memory Verses: Ephesians 4:11-13

Overview

Now that you have covered five basic issues in the discipleship course, we will go into topics that are more involved and more likely to cause controversy. You cannot avoid facing difficult issues with a new Christian. You should not want to avoid them; since a new Christian will have to wrestle with hard questions throughout his Christian life, he might as well learn to approach them properly from the outset.

These last three topics concern a new Christian's interaction with and influence upon other people. While Christian discipleship is never finished in this life, there is a reasonable goal for a basic discipleship course such as this one. That goal is *to make the new Christian a disciple maker.* Encourage him to take everything that he has learned and give it to someone else! He should witness to others and teach them the basics of the Christian faith. With another copy of the same booklet you used, he could lead some other new or immature Christian to learn the foundational beliefs of the Christian faith.

Likewise, he should become an active participant in a local church ministry. He should dedicate himself to do whatever God wants. He should establish solid habits that help him grow as a Christian, including a regular time for personal Bible study. As you read the following section, place yourself in the shoes of a new Christian by imagining that you are hearing these truths for the first time.

Witnessing–Talking about God

What is a witness? A witness is one who has seen and heard something and has been called to testify about it before others.

One of the last things Jesus said before He ascended into heaven after His resurrection was, "Ye shall be witnesses" (Acts 1:8). The early church took this to heart, and Christianity grew rapidly.

The responsibility to be a witness for Christ is every bit as heavy upon us today as it was in the first century. You may feel that you have not studied the Bible enough to witness effectively, but if you are a Christian, you can at least give someone else the testimony of how you were saved. The blind man in John 9 did not know much about Jesus either, but he knew that he had been changed. He said to the Pharisees, "Whether he [Jesus] be a sinner or no, I know not: one thing I know, that, whereas I was blind, now I see" (v. 25).

That simple testimony is enough for a start, but you will need to become familiar with Bible verses that will lend authority to what you say. You will find some verses effective for evangelistic purposes in the back of this book. Insert these verses into your personal testimony as you witness. Become familiar with the brief explanation of each verse given below.

Romans 3:23   This verse means everyone has sinned. No one has measured up to God's standard of holiness.

Romans 6:23   Because of our sin we deserve to spend eternity separated from God in hell–eternal death.

Ephesians 2:8-9   There is nothing we can do to save ourselves. Salvation is a gift from God.

John 3:16   God's great love for us caused Him to send His Son to die in our place and suffer our hell for us.

John 1:12   We must believe Christ died for us and personally receive Him to have eternal life.

Isaiah 55:7   God expects that if a man truly desires to be saved, he will turn from sin at the same time he turns to God.

1. What does Jesus promise to give you that will encourage you as you witness (Matt. 28:20*b*)?

2. What did the early church pray for (Acts 4:29)?

3. Why is it so important to keep your life clean (Matt. 5:16)?

4. What are two results of leading someone to Christ (James 5:20)?

   a.
   b.

5. What does God say about the man who "wins souls" (tries to lead people to Christ) (Prov. 11:30*b*)?

Begin reading good books on soulwinning and become active in your church visitation program. Take every opportunity that God gives to tell others what God has done for you.

For additional help on talking about God, study the personal witnessing of Christ in John 3 as He talked with Nicodemus and in John 4 as He talked with the woman at the well.

Church Attendance–Meeting with God's People

In Acts 2:42 the Bible says that the new Christians "continued stedfastly in the apostles' doctrine [solid biblical teaching] and fellowship." These two elements are essential to Christian growth. God has established the local church as the means to meet these needs. Some today would scorn meeting together in an organized fashion. It is true that some churches have nothing to offer the believer who is seeking to be fed from God's Word, but God has not abandoned this institution. Of course, a Christian must use caution in selecting the right kind of church. God has chosen to use the church to build up His people. As long as a church stands true to God's Word, God will bless it and protect it.

1. According to Ephesians 4:11, God has set up certain types of Christian workers. One of these is the pastor. Verse 12 expresses the reason for his work. What is his purpose?

2. What is the pastor's responsibility according to Acts 20:28?

3. Some of the early believers in New Testament times had a certain problem. What was it (Heb. 10:25)?

4. As Acts 2:42 points out, "fellowship" is essential to Christian growth. What benefit of fellowship does Ecclesiastes 4:9-10 describe?

5. What is another benefit of Christian fellowship (Heb. 10:24)?

6. What is the proper attitude toward church (Ps. 122:1)?

7. In contrast to fellowship with Christians, what is to be our response to ungodly friends (Prov. 4:14)?

8. Proverbs 13:20 says "He that walketh with wise men shall be wise." What does the rest of this verse say is the end of the man who does not seek Christian fellowship?

Although it is important to attend church, a young believer must be selective in the church he attends. The Bible gives definite instructions as to the kind of church a Christian should fellowship with.

Matthew 28:19-20—Its members must be concerned about reaching the unsaved for Christ both at home and around the world.

I Corinthians 15:3-4—It must have the gospel as its central message. This means its pastor and teachers will continually be telling their listeners how to be saved. They will offer regular times of "invitation" when a person can get help on how to be saved.

I Timothy 3:1-13—Its leaders should meet God's qualifications of dedication and holy living.

II Corinthians 6:14, 17—It should be independent of ungodly alliances and associations with religious organizations that do not obey the Bible or that do not hold it to be entirely true (inerrant).

Churches that meet these qualifications often describe themselves as "independent," "fundamental," and "evangelistic." Once you have found the right church, get involved in the soulwinning activities and attend all the services. God has raised up churches such as these to strengthen you spiritually through biblical preaching and teaching and through fellowship with other believers who love and obey the Bible as you do.

Dedication–Surrendering to God's Will

Once you repent of your sin and accept Jesus Christ as your Savior, you should soon realize that you are not your own. You belong to God. The apostle Paul said it this way:

> "What? know ye not that your body is the temple of the Holy Ghost which is in you, which ye have of God, and ye are not your own? For ye are bought with a price: therefore glorify God in your body, and in your spirit, which are God's."
>
> I Corinthians 6:19-20

According to I Peter 1:18-19, what are we purchased with?

In Romans 12:1, Paul states that God wants us to present (give over) our bodies as a living sacrifice to Him. The picture Paul portrays here brings to mind the Old Testament sacrifices where an animal was killed and offered to God. Paul is saying that we are to be dead (sacrificed), yet "living." We are to be alive physically, yet we are to consider ourselves dead to our flesh (our sinful nature). Romans 6:11 teaches this idea as well.

> "Likewise reckon [consider] ye also yourselves to be dead indeed unto sin, but alive unto God through Jesus Christ our Lord."

God wants you to allow Him to totally control your body. He also wants to control what you do with your life since He owns you.

If you have not done so before, now would be a good time to bow your head and tell God that you want Him to have full control of you from this time on—you are now presenting your body to Him as a "living sacrifice." Also, tell Him you recognize that since He bought you, He owns you; thus, you will do anything He wants you to do. This decision is called dedication.

After you have decided to surrender your body and life to God in this way, you will want to ask yourself, "What does God want me to do with my life now?" Several considerations are suggested for you below.

A. Ask yourself, "What can I do for Christ now?"

    1. List the opportunities in your church where you may be able to serve (helping with the youth program, visiting shut-ins, driving a bus, and so forth).

    2. List the abilities, skills, and talents that you have that can be used for God now.

    3. In what ways can you be a testimony for Christ? At home? At work? At school?

B. Ask yourself, "What can I do for Christ in the future?"

    1. Has God placed on your heart a burden for a particular type of work or Christian service? If so, what is it?

    2. Are you willing to serve God anywhere?

    3. Do you need additional educational preparation?

    Note: Often someone who has recently been saved finds it helpful to prepare for service at a Christian school. If you think this might be what the Lord has for you, write to the address on page 24 and ask for information on obtaining Christian education.

In Proverbs 3:5-6 God promises to "direct your paths" if you "acknowledge him in all your ways." God bless you as you seek to find and do His will.

For additional help about surrendering to God's will, see Luke 9:23-26.

*A*dditional Helps for Christian Growth

A Plan for a Daily Quiet Time with God

Nothing will help you grow more and build your relationship with God more quickly than a daily quiet time. This is a time when you meet with God. Remember the following points as you begin to make this a part of your schedule.

1. Establish a regular time. Many Christians find that early morning is best since meeting with God early ensures that their first thoughts will be of spiritual things (Ps. 5:3).

2. Get alone. Shut yourself up in a room away from the distractions of people (Matt. 6:6).

3. Have a pen and notebook ready. Proverbs 10:14*a* says, "Wise men lay [store] up knowledge." Be ready to write down anything that God points out to you from His Word.

You should include the following elements in your quiet time:

A. Bible Reading

Pray before you begin reading. Ask God to show you something just for yourself (Ps. 119:18).

Follow a Bible reading schedule so that your reading is not haphazard. Some find that including the chapter of Proverbs that corresponds to the day of the month is helpful too. For example, read Proverbs 15 on the fifteenth day of the month, and so on.

Read until God points out something especially for you. Jot down the verse and your immediate thoughts about it. As you read, God will convict you of sins in your life. Write down your decision to forsake these sins. Confess these to God and ask for power to overcome them in your prayer time. God uses His Word to cleanse us (John 15:3).

Thank God for what He has shown you in your reading.

Share these special verses and insights with others (I John 1:3).

B. Meditation—4M Formula

Mark verses in your Bible from the "Verses for Victory" section or from your own Bible reading, and write them out on cards to carry with you.

Memorize these verses in free moments during the day (Ps. 119:11).

Meditate on one verse or passage for a few minutes during your quiet time (Ps. 1:2-3). In meditation you are thinking of applications of these verses to your life. You are "personalizing" God's Word.

Master these Bible truths in your daily life. God will bring opportunities into your life for you to "exercise" and grow stronger (Heb. 5:14).

C. Prayer—Keeping a Personal Prayer Journal

Our prayers to God should contain a balance of praise, confession, thanksgiving, and supplication (asking). You can keep this balance by letting the little word "ACT" remind you of these elements. Begin your daily prayer time by "ACTing." Memorize the Scripture passages following each element and pray them back to God from the depths of your heart.

Adoring God for who He is (Ps. 8; I Chron. 29:11-13)

Confessing your sin (I John 1:9; Ps. 32:1-5)

Thanking Him for what He has done (Ps. 100:4)

Then, you may ask God to act. This is the time when you "let your requests be made known unto God" (Phil. 4:6).

A balanced prayer life has times of fellowship with God (this is when you "ACT") and times of petition to God for help. Our tendency is to forget the times of adoration and thanksgiving. Without them, however, our prayer life becomes a shallow "give me" time. Your times of adoration and thanksgiving will become easier as you see God answer your requests. Of course, this does not mean that every time you pray you must include all four elements, but none of them should be missing from your regular prayer life. If you wish, use the Personal Prayer Journal in the supplement to help you get started. A Bible Reading Schedule for the New Testament is on the reverse side of the Prayer Journal. This reading schedule will help keep you consistent. If you are a new Christian, begin by reading I John, the Gospel of John, and James; then go back and finish the rest of the New Testament. Write the date you read the passage in the box in front of the day's assignment. After you have read the entire New Testament, secure a schedule for the whole Bible and read the Bible through yearly.

Verses for Victory

Forgiveness	I John 1:9	Ps. 103:12	I John 2:1-2
Patience	Heb. 10:36	James 1:2-4	I Pet. 2:20
Strength	Eph. 3:16	Phil. 4:13	Eph. 6:10-11
Lust (1)	II Tim. 2:22	I John 2:15-17	I Pet. 2:11
Lust (2)	Matt. 5:28	Rom. 13:14	James 1:15
Priorities	Matt. 6:33	Acts 20:24	Phil. 3:8
Self-Discipline	Eccl. 5:4	Luke 9:23	James 1:19-20
Pleasing God	Matt. 6:24	Eph. 6:6-7	Col. 3:23
Christian Walk	Eph. 4:1-2	Eph. 5:2	Eph. 5:8-9
Temptation	I Cor. 10:13	James 4:7	Rom. 6:11-13
Peace	John 14:27	John 16:33	Phil. 4:6-7
Wise Counsel	Prov. 11:14	Prov. 12:15	Prov. 1:5
Courage	Ps. 31:24	Ps. 34:4	Prov. 29:25
Pride (1)	Prov. 16:18	Rom. 12:3	James 4:6
Pride (2)	Obad. 1:4	Matt. 20:26-27	I Cor. 4:7
Love	Deut. 6:5	John 13:35	John 15:13
Worldliness	Rom. 12:2	Col. 3:2	James 4:4
Tongue	James 3:6	Eph. 4:29	Prov. 10:19
Lying	Ps. 120:2	Ps. 101:7	Prov. 19:5
Stealing	Eph. 4:28	Prov. 30:8-9	Exod. 20:15
Suffering	Rom. 8:18	Phil. 1:29	I Pet. 2:21
Church Attendance	Ps. 122:1	Matt. 18:20	Heb. 10:25
Evil Thoughts	II Cor. 10:5	Phil. 4:8	Eph. 5:12
Critical Spirit	I Cor. 10:10	Phil. 2:14	James 5:9
Strong Drink	Isa. 5:11	Hab. 2:15	Rom. 14:21
Guidance	Prov. 3:5-6	Ps. 32:8	Prov. 1:23
Forgiving Others	Matt. 5:44	Mark 11:25	Eph. 4:32
Knowing God	Jer. 9:23-24	John 17:3	Phil. 3:8-10
Assurance	John 3:36	John 10:28	I John 5:13

As you find other areas of need and Verses for Victory, write them in the space below.

Personal Prayer Journal

Include these elements in your regular prayer time.

   I. Include a time when you "ACT."

       Adoring God for who He is (Ps. 8; I Chron. 29:11-13)

       Confessing your sin (I John 1:9; Ps. 32:1-5)

       Thanking Him for what He has done (Ps. 100:4)

  II. Include a time when you ask God to "act" (Phil. 4:6). (Write these requests in the spaces below.)

Date Requested	Request	Date Answered

Memory Verses

1. Assurance

   "He that believeth on the Son hath everlasting life: and he that believeth not the Son shall not see life; but the wrath of God abideth on him." John 3:36

2. Assurance

   "And I give unto them eternal life; and they shall never perish, neither shall any man pluck them out of my hand." John 10:28

3. We are all sinners

   "For all have sinned, and come short of the glory of God." Romans 3:23

4. The penalty of sin

   "For the wages of sin is death; but the gift of God is eternal life through Jesus Christ our Lord." Romans 6:23

5. We cannot save ourselves

   "For by grace are ye saved through faith; and that not of yourselves: it is the gift of God: Not of works, lest any man should boast." Ephesians 2:8-9

6. Christ died for us

   "For God so loved the world, that he gave his only begotten Son, that whosoever believeth in him should not perish, but have everlasting life." John 3:16

7. We must believe on Christ

   "But as many as received him, to them gave he power to become the sons of God, even to them that believe on his name." John 1:12

8. We must turn from sin

   "Let the wicked forsake his way, and the unrighteous man his thoughts: and let him return unto the Lord, and he will have mercy upon him; and to our God, for he will abundantly pardon." Isaiah 55:7

Review Questions

True or False

_____1. God's promises to answer our prayers are uncondi-
    tional.

_____2. I Corinthians 6:19-20 implies a person can be saved but
    not be glorifying God with his body.

Short/Long Answer

3. What verse from the section "Prayer—Talking With God"
   in Chapter 4 does a disciple who says "God just doesn't
   seem real to me" need to understand and believe?

4. Remembering Chapter 1 of this book, which verse from
   "Witnessing" will be the hardest for your disciple to get unsaved people to believe? Why?

5. According to the questions in "Church Attendance," list five
   benefits a new convert will receive from a good church.
   Include the Scripture references.

_____6. What is the best way for a new convert with little Bible knowledge to witness to others?

    A. Sharing his personal testimony

    B. Passing out tracts

    C. Preaching on street corners

    D. Waiting to witness until he learns more about the Bible.

_____7. Which of the following comments from a new believer would most likely indicate that the church he attends does not meet the qualifications set down in "Church Attendance"?

    A. "It seems like every month there is another sermon on how to get saved!" (see I Corinthians 15:3-4)

    B. "Those people seem totally preoccupied with witnessing!" (see Matthew 28:19-20)

    C. "The pastor told me that the Bible never says anything about drinking!" (see I Timothy 3:1-13)

    D. None of these

8. Explain in your own words what gives God the right to tell you what to do with your whole life.

9-10. Suppose someone you are discipling shows you this prayer journal after his first week of regular devotions. Write one thing to praise him for and two problems you see that he needs to work on.

Date	Bible	Application	Request	Answer
4/6	Prov 6	A proud look is wrong	Help me find a better job	Yes
4/7	Prov 7	Prostitution is evil	Help me find a good mechanic	Didn't
4/8	Prov 8	Wisdom is important	Show me if I should quit this job.	
4/9	Prov 9	Don't correct a mocker	Good weather this Saturday	No
4/10	Prov 10	Don't talk too much	Get my boss to leave	

Notes

Notes

Notes

Notes